AUTOPILOT INVESTING

MAKE YOUR MONEY SOAR USING FOUR
CONCEPTS YOU'VE ALREADY MASTERED

SCOTT MCGURK

AUTOPILOT INVESTING

TABLE OF CONTENTS

About Scott

Scott McGurk is an airline pilot, opportunistic investor, husband and father. During his early career as an airline pilot he found his other passions, real estate investing and teaching.

After spending several years studying the real estate industry, Scott started investing in multifamily properties in June 2017. That year he also founded Blue Side Up Capital, which provides an opportunity for airline pilots and other individuals to invest in value-added and stabilized commercial properties.

His passion for teaching led to the creation of the Multifamily Masters Indianapolis Chapter Meetup. This monthly meetup focuses on finding, analyzing and managing multifamily properties. Scott also speaks about the importance of financial literacy and what actions we can take to fulfill our goals.

Why I Wrote This Book

I see too many pilots and other professionals failing to take off when it comes to their retirement and wealth generation. We are frozen with fear of making the wrong decision about our 401Ks, IRAs and retirement accounts. Because of this, we do nothing other than play it safe!

I've heard too many times that, "I'm just going to invest my retirement so that I can live off of a conservative 2-3% return." There is so much more you can be doing with your money.

All of us have seen our money disappear from the stock market either in the dot-com bubble, real estate bubble, or both! It is time we stepped out of our comfort zone to reach our retirement goals.

I hope that you'll find inspiration and real, actionable ideas that will help you do more and take control of your financial future. Remember, nobody cares as much about you as you.

"Be comfortable with conflict. You often have to fail to succeed."
SCOTT MCGURK

My Story

There are two sides to my story, the aviation side and the investor side. I share that with you because it's important for you to know that even if you're busy, even if you think you are years from retirement, you can start today laying the groundwork for your financial future.

I started flying during the summer of 2003 before my freshman year at Indiana State University's Aviation Program. Indiana State is also where I built up my flight time with instruction at Hulman Field.

In early 2007, after college, I started flying for Trans State Airlines on the Embraer 145. Flying at a regional airline is one of those jobs you never forget. The pay sucks! Being gone from home all the time sucks! Staying at the cheapest hotel sucks! But man, you work with some great people.

As you may know, the airline industry has its ups and downs. It's one of those industries that is first to downsize in an economic contraction. My first experience with this was in April 2009 when I was furloughed. I went from being a few slots away from upgrading to captain, to being laid off seven months later.

During that time, I became a car salesman just to make ends meet until I could get back into an aviation job. Thankfully I was picked up by Republic Airways as a pilot ground instructor, and later transitioned into their safety department as an FOQA analyst. I stayed in the office until 2012 when I was able to get back into flying once again on the Embraer 170 aircraft.

In 2016, I had the pleasure of joining one of the big three legacy airlines in the country, which shall remain nameless, where I currently fly on one of their domestic fleets.

As I sit down to put the final touches on this book, we are in the middle of the COVID-19 pandemic. I am once again reminded of the importance of financial literacy and always being prepared. Don't sit on the sidelines, clueless and watch your future evaporate! No one cares more about your money than you! Start taking action today!

2008

Negative 35%

That's the return I was making on my 401k in the fall of 2008.

As an airline pilot, I've consistently made strategic, educated decisions to succeed throughout my life and in my career. So when I saw a negative 35 percent return on my 401k statement, I was angry and almost felt betrayed.

I'd done everything I'd been told I was supposed to do to steadily grow my wealth and be prepared for retirement.

Why wasn't I seeing results I was promised?

"Damn, I need to find a wealth strategy I can control," I remember realizing.

2009

One year later, my stomach dropped as I received the news I'd been furloughed. As a pilot, my job comes with unknown circumstances. I always assumed I would be financially prepared when it happened, but I wasn't thinking it would happen yet.

2010 - 2017

I wasted seven years studying the topic of commercial real estate investing rather than taking action and putting my money where my brain (and the countless sources I'd been researching) were telling me to.

The support and means to start investing were always there—whether I realized it or not—but I kept putting it off, waiting until I felt fully "qualified."

After all, apartment investing is for rich people—those seasoned professionals who know everything there is to know about real estate...right?

Wrong.

2017

I took action! I built up a team. I started investing, I watched my equity steadily grow and the idea of retirement become less and less daunting, and eventually, I founded Blue Side Up Capital to help other pilots do the same.

The aviation industry experiences the same ups and downs as the stock market. So, as airline pilots, our jobs come with inherent risk.

This means we need cash flow coming from multiple sources, rather than staking our families current and future lives on our one monthly paycheck along with an underfunded pension system and uncertain retirement plans.

Realizing our financial future may not be as inherently bright as we'd initially anticipated can be intimidating. That's why it can be easy to be tempted by the get-rich-quick methods every uncle, buddy, or long-lost family friend seems to be tossing our way once they learn we've added a zero to our income.

And investing in assets like real estate can perhaps feel risky as well or like a challenge you're unqualified for. But, apartment investing is a team sport. With the right teammates, it doesn't all land on your shoulders.

As a legacy airline pilot with twelve years of experience, I'm no stranger to teamwork. I work with amazing individuals to get the aircraft off the

ground and safely back home every
day.

After realizing investing in commercial real estate to secure my financial future engages similar partnerships, I formed a great team of investors that works with Blue Side Up Capital.

Chapter 1: Lift

Everything is your fault.

How does that statement make you feel? Does it make you defensive? Get your back up? Trigger your fight or flight response?

Now, take a deep breath and look at that statement again. This time, forget the blame game going on in your head. Forget the attachment you have to the words themselves.

Everything is your fault.

- Where you are in life.
- What you do for a living.
- Where you live.
- Who you love.
- The car you drive.
- The house you live in.
- The clothes you wear.
- Where you went (or didn't go) on vacation.
- How much money is in your bank account.
- Your relationship status.
- When you'll retire.
- It's all up to you.

That is a hard thing for most of us to consider. It is so much easier to blame your parents, your circumstances, the opportunities that did (or didn't) come your way.

One of the most important things you can do to make real, lasting change in your life is to take personal responsibility for everything. Let me say that again. EVERYTHING.

You see, many of us are perfectly happy to take responsibility for some of the things that have happened in our lives. We can all see times when we made a bad decision or hung out with the wrong person.

It's so much harder to take real, serious, personal responsibility for everything that has happened in our lives. How-ever, once you do it, you're free.

Free to

- Try new things
- Accomplish more
- Take actions every day
- Let go of past trauma
- Move forward in your life.

How can you take more responsibility for your own success?

Financial Literacy

If you don't know much about finances -- whether personal or professional -- it's important for you to start learning about financial literacy.

There are a variety of resources available to you online to help you, including articles, videos, podcasts, and more. Get smart and study up about

- Budgets
- Taxes
- Profit and Loss
- Insurance
- Retirement Planning
- Equity
- Leverage

Maybe you have an advanced degree but couldn't find a position in your chosen field. Maybe you barely made it through high school.

You made choices every day of your educational career. There's still time to do more, if that is your goal.

You don't have to apply for an Executive MBA program. Maybe you should start with a bookkeeping class. Maybe a marketing class would help you figure out how to promote your business.

A real estate licensure program, an appraisal workshop, training in home inspections -- any of these can pay big benefits and make you a more effective investor.

Take a look at how education can create leverage in your business, and find out how to get the information you need to create the business you want.

Mentors

You are known by the company you keep. When you surround yourself with smart people, people who are farther down the path you want to go down, you create powerful leverage for your business.

A great mentor can save you years in mistakes, losses, and frustrating setbacks. Get to know someone who is 5-10 years further along the road than you are, then learn from them.

Up-Reach

Get connected with people who are already doing what you'd like to do, then make connections and absorb some of their hard-earned knowledge.

This is different from a mentorship -- less personal, shorter term -- but can still pay big dividends in helping you learn the ropes of real estate investment and finance.

The idea here is to learn from people who are just a few years further along than you are. They've made some of those first-timer mistakes -- and their insights can help you avoid those.

Continue to up-reach, always looking for someone who's just a little more experienced than you are so that you'll always have that next-level knowledge on hand.

Your "Guy." As a real estate investor, you need

- A finance "guy"
- A title and settlement "guy"
- A legal "guy"
- A deal-finding "guy"
- A marketing "guy"
- A construction "guy"

It doesn't matter whether your "guy" is a guy or a girl, you need a team on your side. Think of it as your executive committee or your advisory board.

You see, you don't have to know everything about every aspect of your business. You need to have access to people who know everything about every aspect of your business.

Creating a team -- and allowing them to guide you -- is an important part of building leverage into your investment strategy. You can draw on the knowledge, skill, and experience of others to help you do more and accomplish more in your investment projects.

Chapter 2: Weight

What is weighing you down and keeping you from experiencing liftoff in your financial life? For many people, it's a combination of self-doubt and negative self-esteem that keeps them from taking action and sustaining that action over the long term.

Have you ever seen the SNL sketch "Debbie Downer?" Debbie Downer is a woman who goes to a happy place or occasion -- like Disney World in one sketch or a wedding in another -- and meets everyone's positive energy with a sad fact or depressing statistic.

The sketch itself is hilarious and the character, played by Rachel Dratch, is, too. However, the impact of this kind of negativity isn't so funny.

Many of us were raised with a lot of toxic messages about money, wealth, and success. Our well-meaning parents and grandparents may have given us messages (directly or indirectly) like the following:

- Money is the root of all evil.
- Rich people are evil/greedy.
- Money doesn't grow on trees.
- Money changes people.
- There's never enough money.

- God doesn't love rich people.
- God only loves rich people.
- Money just buys more troubles.
- Wealth is an illusion; it can all disappear.

The list is practically endless, and many of us end up with a screwed-up view of money because of that early training from family members or religious leaders who either lived in lack and scarcity or obsessed over money and how to get more of it.

What is money?

In reality, of course, money is a unit of measure, a means of exchange. That dollar bill in your pocket is no different from some shiny beads or bits of glass that older civilizations used as a stand-in for value.

While many of our negative beliefs about money have to do with changes that it creates in people, in reality, money just amplifies who you already are. If you are unscrupulous, a lot of money will probably make you even more shifty.

If you are generous, a lot of money will allow you to put those generous impulses to work to help more people than you ever thought possible.

If you are creative, a lot of money will help fund your creative endeavors, allowing you plenty of room and time to expand your thinking and pursue your passions.

If you are family-oriented, a lot of money can help you take care of your family like never before, fund family vacations and holiday celebrations, and allow you to leave a financial legacy behind for your children and grandchildren.

Stop letting false messages and false information define your relationship with money. Stop thinking of money as the angel on your shoulder or the demon on your shoulder.

Instead, use money as a tool in order to fund the lifestyle you want.

There's a great book called *You Are a Badass at Making Money* by Jen Sincero. In it she says,

"The good news is if you, like most people, have a troubled or conflicted relationship with money, you have the ability to heal it, transform it, and become such awesome pals with money that you wake up one day to find yourself standing in the middle of the life you've always wanted to live."

That's what I want for you. Forget fear and shame and just make the money you need to live the life you want. It's that easy -- and that difficult.

Chapter 3:Thrust

Making progress toward your goals can be a challenge. You may feel like you need more answers, but in reality, you really need to ask yourself the right questions.

Why?

Finding out your "why" is an important part of determining what motivates you and keeps you on track.

- Why do you get up in the morning?
- Why do you work hard?
- Why do you want to succeed?
- Why do you want to earn more money?
- Why do you want to leave a legacy behind?

Maybe it's for your family. Maybe it's for your own sense of purpose. Maybe you want to retire early and travel the world.

Maybe you want to leave an endowment to your favorite university or non-profit.

There is no "right" answer to "Why?" There's just your answer.

Who?

Who speaks to you? Whose voice do you hear when you get discouraged or when you need inspiration?

The messages you surround yourself with determine your mindset. Seek out positive voices and messages and you'll change your inner monologue.

Some of the best motivational and inspirational writers and speakers out there are:

- Tony Robbins
- Grant Cardone
- Dan Pena
- Zig Zigler

- Eckhart Tolle
- Brené Brown
- Rachel Hollis
- Rick Warren
- Jack Canfield
- Gary Vaynerchuk
- Tim Ferris
- Les Brown
- Daymond John
- Simon Sinek

Check out their books, including audiobooks. Listen to podcasts. Choose your favorite quotes and surround yourself with them. Start your day with affirmations.

Change your headspace and you change your life.

Also, figure out which motivational speaker speaks to you in your "language." You don't have to listen to all of the speakers I listed above to become successful. Pick a few of them that really speak to you and go for it.

Personally, I need the type of motivation you get from a high school football coach. He comes running up to me cussing up a storm, points out exactly how I screwed up, slaps me in the helmet and tells me to get back in there!

I don't need the type of speaker that wants me to get in touch with my feelings or write a journal entry. That doesn't move the needle for me.

What?

Starting your day the right way is the secret to optimum performance. One of my favorite rituals is from Hal Elrod, author of *Miracle Morning*. It's a great way to build self-esteem and mental toughness.

It's called SAVERS, which stands for the following:

Silence

Whether it's prayer, meditation, or just listening to your breathing, starting your day with silence helps you learn to focus and begin your day from a peaceful place.

Affirmations

Speak encouragement, bravery, and strength to yourself with affirmative statements that help reinforce your goals and your purpose.

Visual

In as much detail as possible, visualize yourself living the life of your dreams. Go step-by-step through the process of moving forward and accomplishing your goals.

Exercise

You don't have to train for a marathon or a weightlifting competition. Do some stretches, bodyweight exercises, or go for a quick walk to get your day started right.

Read

Read an inspirational book, a business book, the biography of someone you admire. Add some new knowledge and new insights to your day as part of your morning routine.

Scribble

Take some time to write your own thoughts through journaling, blogging, or other writing. This is a great way to help you put together ideas, process input from your reading, and record your insights.

One thing I did want to emphasize from this is meditation. Being an analytic-minded person I never took meditation seriously but boy was I wrong. You can read about the benefits elsewhere but the best way I can describe it is meditation has turned down all the noise in the background. You no longer run around with ten tabs open on your internal internet browser. You are only focused on one, maybe two of those tabs now.

How?

Once you have put these good habits into place and filled your mind with positive thoughts, it's time for the most important part of your process: Taking Action!

Many people get stuck in the input phase of change, spending months or even years on research and planning. They read every book and blog, listen to every podcast, and constantly wait for the right moment, the moment when they'll be really ready.

Ultimately, however, knowing everything and reading everything is no replacement for action.

Understanding the theory behind alternative finance is no substitute for talking to lenders.

Understanding the theory behind marketing is no substitute for geographic farming.

Understanding the theory behind investment is no substitute for finding your first deal.

Give yourself a max of three months to think about things and research things. Then, it's time to get to work.

Start out by making a phone call to someone in the market. Take a meeting. Attend a networking event. Get yourself out there, have conversations, and start learning about real estate investing in real life.

Next, solve a problem. Maybe you need to figure out what market to start farming for deals. Maybe you need to figure out your financing. Maybe you need to walk through a house with another investor to see what he looks for and looks at.

Next, solve a bigger problem. Develop a marketing plan for the farm you identified. Put together financing for your first property. Purchase your first in-vestment property.

Next, solve a bigger problem. Expand your marketing and farming. Develop a financing plan for multiple properties.

Scale up your portfolio or diversify it with duplexes, triplexes, and quads.

Think of your investment portfolio as a series of escalating challenges. Starting it, growing it, optimizing it, diversifying it -- you'll learn from each part of the journey the skills you need to for the next part.

Chapter 4: Drag

What is standing in the way of your success? What is keeping you from getting a handle on your finances and making your goals a reality?

I've identified the top five blocks to real, impactful progress. See if any (or all) of these resonate with you.

If it's true that we are the sum total of the five people we spend the most time with, family and friends may be at the top of your list of problematic people.

Are you trying to be smart about money while the people in your life are constantly in debt, out of work, or otherwise struggling financially? Do your family and friends say things like:

- You're working too hard.
- Why are you so stressed out?
- Don't you have enough to do without taking on a new project?

- You've got a good job. Why worry about money?
- Everything will work out somehow.

This type of "helpful" advice often comes from people who don't understand your goals and ambition. They think that if they are satisfied with less, you should be, too.

Start surrounding yourself with people who teach you, who inspire you, and who uplift you. It's the best way to help you get where you want to go.

Many of us have the "disease to please." We want to be the good son or daughter, the perfect parent, and the perfect partner.

Because of that, it may be hard for us to say "no" to other people.

- No to working an extra flight.
- No to coaching the Little League team.
- No to an out-of-town family obligation.

Don't get me wrong: you need to have some balance in your life. But the reality is, when you are trying to make some-thing big happen in your life, you're going to have to say no sometimes. You're going to disappoint people and you're sometimes going to frustrate them. It's not fun, but it's part of what it takes to prioritize yourself.

Look at some of those people who expect you to drop everything and do what they want you to do. How often do they return the favor? How much do they have going on?

Often, it's clear that the people who expect us to help them only ask us because they know that we're an easy mark. Don't let people take advantage of you, your time, or your good nature.

Say "No," and put yourself first, for a change.

There are people who live in a perpetual state of crisis. They move from relationship to relationship, always looking for the excitement of pursuit or the first kiss.

There are people who live in a perpetual state of anger. They hold grudges and shoot their mouth off at any pro-vocation.

There are people who live in a perpetual state of anxiety. They obsess over the news and work themselves up over events that have nothing to do with them.

There are people who live in a perpetual state of gloominess. They see the worst in everyone and in every situation and convince themselves that they are powerless.

If you are being ruled by your emotions, you'll find ways to fuel the drama. It's like a feedback loop -- the more heightened your emotional state the more drama you crave.

Rather than pursuing the artificial excitement of high school drama, pursue the genuine excitement of accomplishment. Try something new. Learn something new. Develop yourself and your skills.

Don't let a taste for drama keep you from doing real, meaningful things in your life.

Similarly, some people are their own worst enemies. They seek out ways to self-sabotage -- subconsciously, of course -- and derail their success before it even gets started.

 There are a variety of reasons for this, including:

- Fear of success
- Fear of failure
- Fear of doing better than your parents
- Fear of out-earning your spouse
- Fear of the future
- Fear of the unknown
- Fear of change

Look back at your life and find the places where you have struggled and failed. Remember Chapter One? Everything is your fault.

What could you have done differently? How did you contribute to your own worst mistakes? In what ways are you creating problems for yourself -- and setting yourself up for failure?

Finally, there are those who don't fail because they don't do anything at all. They are constantly reading just one more book or listening to just one more podcast. They think that if they work at it long enough, they can think through every eventuality to inevitable success.

Here's the thing. There's a certain amount of risk in everything. If you spend all of your time trying to see around corners and be ten steps ahead, you'll never take that first step.

Overthinking isn't smart. It isn't savvy. It's an excuse for doing nothing at all. It's cowardice disguised as research. And it will never get you one step closer to your goals.

Think. Study. Research. But at some point, get up and move.

Pick up the phone.

Make the appointment.

Knock on the door.

Do something.

What Now?

There is opportunity out there -- no matter what. Whatever the market looks like. Whatever the news is saying. No matter who's President. It's there. *The question is, what will you do next?*

Here's what I'd like for you to do. Give me a call. Let's discuss what is holding you back from taking off. Let's discuss what else you could be doing with your money. My company is Blue Side Up Capital, and we're here to help. Here's how to get in touch:

smcgurk@bluesideupcapital.com